A Date with the Soulmate

- An Emotional Instinct

notionpress.com

A Date with the Soulmate

- An Emotional Instinct

Suresh K Agarwal

notionpress.com

Notion Press

5 Muthu Kalathy Street, Triplicane,

Chennai - 600 005

First Published by Notion Press 2014

ISBN: 978-93-83808-88-5

A Date with the Soulmate
An Emotional Instinct

Inspired by	-	B.P. Agarwal
Motivated by	-	Santosh Agarwal
Authored by	-	Suresh K Agarwal
Concept by	-	Manju Agarwal
Creation by	-	Devashish Agarwal
Compiled by	-	Divit Agarwal
Admired by	-	Khushali Agarwal
Loved by	-	One and All

The Book

The contents of the book are life inspirational, motivators and full of moral values and ethics. The purpose of the book shall serve as a handy ready reckonner and correct the mistakes of life and never fail and always succeed without any ego. Innocence is the flavour of the book which is adorable area very lovely and god willing will be liked by all ages readers - including children's because the small moral stories read and listened have been crafted on almost all the grounds of life from - Greed, Luck, Fear, Proud, Be what you are etc. The journey of the book will be very heart touching to the readers because its all about ups and downs of life, comforts and pains of life, success and failures, innocence and over confidence. The main reason behind the contents of the chapter is to live life with principles of life, with some dignity with some efforts, without any fear, pain, hurt, love the life as it comes and do the best and leave the rest is the mantra of the book. The karma theory is also scripted without the influences of false Ego of the doer's activities in the chapters.

The Author

The author is a God fearing man with sensitive and emotional nature. The author has given his best out of his life's experiences which he has gone through from good and bad, ups and downs, breakthru and breakdown finances, Deteriorated Relationships, Passion and Compassions, Success and failures, Comforts and Sufferings, Innocence and overconfidence and ultimately practically faced and learned the subjects in reality and morals and philosophies of life, Ethics and principles of Business are the contents of the book.

This is for all the generations to correct themselves and not to suffer and commit the same mistakes and prosper and lead a life with dignity and die with dignity.

The people who bank on only luck will also not benefit and will waste their precious time waiting for windfalls. The efforts and luck runs parallel like the rail-track equally. The author is also a firm believer of karma theory – Do the best and live the rest. And keep on doing without any expectations of the results of your doings. Play the character of the show to your best, you will be awarded, you will be rewarded, you will be applauded. Under the influence of false ego one thinks himself to be the doer of activities, while in reality all activities are carried out by nature as natural process.

The author has seen the riches and spent lavishly on comforts; clothes, luxury cars and was the frequent flyer and was the privilege card holder of all the airlines, and at the same time he never felt to move on with a two wheeler, with no credit cards. No bank balances, no protocols absolutely a medicore life.

The author has passed through severe depression stage when his industries were shutdown, auctioned by bankers and was imprisoned for 45 days for charges of tax evasion for amassing wealth in a short term by the authorities. Therefore ability without dependability, responsibility and flexibility is a liability.

People without conviction do not take a stand– They go along to get along because they lack confidence and courage. Some people consider themselves a shade better because they do not support the wrong, however they lack the conviction to oppose. But by not opposing something you know is wrong, you are actually supporting it. And here I end up by saying –

"If you can you will and If you can't you will never."

And

Finally my inspirational lines which aspired me to write –

"If you write something it should be worth reading and if can't, then do something worth writing"

- See more at: https://notionpress.com/read/a-date-with-the soulmate#sthash.6lWeZAGR.dpuf

Contents

Golden Words (Quotes)

If you fail to plan, you are planning to fail.
Planning without action is futile.
Action without planning is fatal.

Success is simple - Do what's right,
the right way at the right time.

No sound in this world can be more louder than silence and if any one cannot understand your silence they can never understand your word.

You have a right to "Karma" (actions) but never to any fruits thereof. You should never be motivated by the results of your actions, nor should there be any attachment in not doing your prescribed activities. (duties).

There are no secrets to success. It is the result of preparation, hard work and learning from the failure. Success does not lower its standard to accommodate us, we have to raise our standard to achieve it!

For every bird God provides food but not nest. You have to build it by yourself, let it take time, it will not be available ready made to you.

When you do anything new, at first people laugh at you, then they challenge you, then they watch you succeed and then they wish they were you.

Our task now is not to fix the blame for the past, but fix the course for the future.

Destiny is not a matter of chance, it is a matter of choice, it is not a thing to be waited for, it is a thing to be achieved.

When your Signature becomes autograph it means - you are successful.

Efforts (Quotes)

He worked by the day. And toiled by the night. He gave up play, And some delight. Dry books he read, New things to learn. And forged ahead, Success to earn. He plodded on with, faith and pluck. And when he won, men called it luck.

ꕥ

I am not the one who bank upon luck, and not afraid of those who rely on it. I see luck as an opportunity to work harder.

ꕥ

"He slept beneath the moon, He basked beneath the sun, He lived a life of going to do, and died with nothing done."

ꕥ

"Achievers never expose themselves, but their achievements expose them, Do or die was an old saying, Do before you die is the new one."

ꕥ

A paper flying in air is due to luck, but a kite flying in air is due to your efforts! So don't worry if luck doesn't support efforts will work.

Luck (Quotes)

Journey of life starts with a full bag of luck and an empty bag of experience. The goal is to fill the bag of experience before the bag of luck gets empty!

ꕥ

You cannot change your future, but you can change your habits. And surely your habits will change your future.

ꕥ

Takdir Ke khel se Nirash nahi hote, Zindagi mein kabhi udas nahi hote, Haath ki lakiro par yakin mat karna, Takdir to unki bhi hoti hai jinke haath nahi hote.

ꕥ

Everything about the future is uncertain, But one thing is sure, God has already arranged all our tomorrows, we just have to trust him today.

ꕥ

Destiny is simply the strength of your desires. If you cry at trouble, it grows double. If you laugh at trouble, it disappears like a bubble. This is how you can be the creator of your own Destiny!

ꕥ

If everything is going according to your wish then you are lucky, if not, then you are too lucky because it is going according to God's wish.

ꕥ

"If you write something it should be worth reading, or if you can't, do something worth writing".

Nobody is Destiny's Child

INFORMATION

(Feedback, Hearing, Knowing, Learning, Understanding, Seeing)

↓

THOUGHTS

(Positive, Negative, Optimist, Pessimist, Practical, Unpractical)

↓

FEELINGS

(Hurt, Pain, Sorrow, Happy, Energetic, Enthusiastic, Overwhelmed)

↓

ACTIONS

(Physical work, verbal, writing, doing, designing, operating)

↓

HABIT

(Repetitive act, daily routine, performing on daily basis, etc),

↓

CHARACTER

(Labeling, judging, analysing, blaming, ethics, morale, principals).

↓

DESTINATION

(Decide to do something, desire to fulfillment/succeed.)

↓

DESTINY

↓

The present is the result of your past, and also the present will be the result of your future. So don't waste your presence, your present is nothing but a happening, which is happening right now. So be in the complete present which is full in itself do not try to attach with your past nor future, it will also spoil your present-past brings tears, future brings fears, whereas the present is the only one who brings cheers! So, enjoy the present which will become past as you enter it and don't worry about future as we don't even know about it, then why to fear. Be always in whole present which is in your hands. Past is like a shooted arrow from a bow, future is stocks of arrow on your back, present is the arrow ready on the bow, now aim it properly on your target and you will reach the goal. If you use your arrow to kill or hurt someone it will get you the same and if you choose to save or relieve someone, it will get you the same result. Life is like a valley, your actions will echo the same. If your hurt somebody, somebody will hurt you and if you save somebody, somebody will save you at the time of pain & sorrow's of life. This is called "Karma theory" that somebody is nobody but you yourself. So the option given to us is the arrow on the bow, use it with utmost care, use it with grace, use it with tactfulness, use it with a kind heart, but not to exhibit your power or skills by hurting the innocent. Do not be influenced by the mind but always listen to your heart. Mind is a plotter and whereas the heart is innocence full of love and sacrifice. If you choose to relieve, you will be relieved from all the pains and sorrow's. Shree Krishna says "Vruthi pravakthi vruthaha" means

- "Thoughts are changed you are relieved from pain". So your thoughts are the seeds to your actions, use judiciously - and one day you will become somebody from nobody and once you become somebody your signature will become autograph - it means you are successful in achieving your goal!

THE LUST FOR COMFORT MURDERS THE PASSION OF THE SOUL

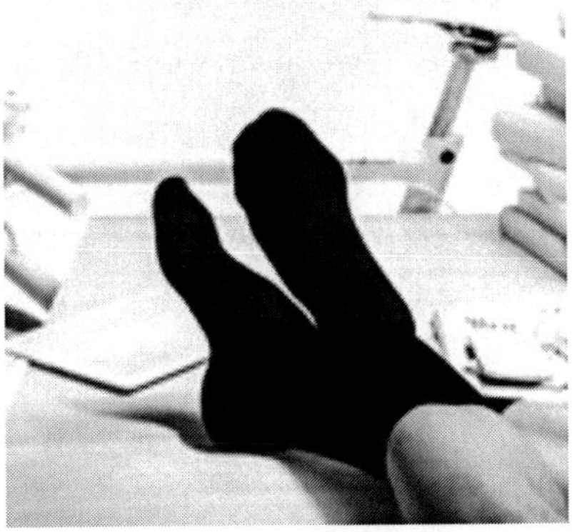

One of my favorite Robin Sharma who noted, "The reasonable man adapts himself to the world; the unreasonable one persists in trying to adapt the world to himself. Therefore all progress depends on the unreasonable man". Please think about that idea for a moment. I suggest it's a big one.

Sure, be practical and operate intelligently as you move through your world. I agree, its important to use common sense. True, foolish risks can lead to difficult consequences. But having said that, don't be so scared of failurc and disappointment that you fail to dream. Don't always be so reasonable and practical and sensible that you refuse to seize glorious opportunities when they show up. Push the envelope as to what's possible for you. Remember critics have always laughed at the visions of bold thinkers and remarkable visionaries. Ignore them. And know that every outstanding piece of human progress was achieved through the heroic efforts of someone who told their ideas was impossible possible to realize. The world needs more dreamers. Unreasonable souls who fight the urge to be ordinary, who resist the seduction of complacency and doing things the way they have always been done. You can be one of them. Beginning today.

The lust for comfort, murders the passion of the soul. The dreamers don't sleep and they work hard without worrying about the results are the real hero's and I salute the heroic efforts of unreasonable man.

BEWARE BITTERNESS-KILLS

People who are affected identify its taste, which is neither sweet nor salty, but bitter - that is why depressions are intrinsically associated to the word "bitterness".

All beings have bitterness in their organism - to a greater or lesser degree - in the same way that almost all of us have the tuberculosis bacillus (T.B). However, these two diseases only attacks when the patient is debilitated; in the case of bitterness, the terrain for the disease to arise appears when we are afraid of the so-called "reality".

Certain people, in their anxiety to build a world where no outside threat could penetrate, increase exaggeratedly their defences against the outside - strangers, new places, different experiences - and leave the inside unprotected. It is then that bitterness begins to cause irreversible harm. People attacked by this evil begin lose their desire for every- thing and in a few years are unable to go outside their world - because they have used up enormous energy reserves building high walls for the reality to be what they wanted it to be. When avoiding outside attack, they also limit internal growth. They continue going to work, watching television, complaining about the traffic and having children, but all that happens automatically, without really understanding why they are behaving like that after all everything is under control. The great problem of bitterness are passions, love, hate, enthusiasm and curiosity which don't appear anymore. The chronically bitter person only notices his disease once a week; on Sunday afternoons. Then, as he has no work or routine to relieve the symptoms, he realises that something is very wrong. However, the cause for the bitterness would not be same for every patient and therefore the treatment cannot be same.

But the medication is only for a good sound sleep, the major therapy is love, affection, attachment, acceptance, counselling, encouraging the number of failures, humiliation, anxiety, tragic moments in life are the major reasons for the cause of this "bitterness" so please be very fragile with the person or he may get hurted though your intention would not be to hurt him. The persons adapt a very narrow side of life and simply take anything and everything to heart their thoughts become very "presumsive" and their perceptions remain "abusive".

Not last but least the critics of the hero's are awarded as "bitterness".

"Forgive the other person but don't forget their name".

CELESTIAL BLISS

Celestial bliss is also known as "Amruth Kalash" the pot of treasures for which Deva's & Asura's were fighting to grab what ever comes out of it one by one, so have a look who got what; and see what you got the most.

Deva's	Asura's
Happiness	Anger
Joyful	Frustration
Satisfaction	Irritation
Love	Fear
Gratitude	Anxiety
Innocence	Greed
Encouragement	Lust
Forgiveness	Guilt
Compassion	Regret
Empathy	Resentment
Creativity	Suffering
Inspiration	Destruction
Motivation	Superiority
Apathy	Comparison
Courage	Jealous
Knowledge	Self Doubt
Devotion	Laziness
Will power	Ego
Enthusiasm	Dominate
Excitement	Lovelessness
Passion	Power greed
Confidence	Blaming
Clarity	Deserted
Sympathy	Hurt
Apologise	Rejected
Cooperation	Betrayal

Coordination	Ignorance
Understanding	Insult
Patience	Humiliation
Serenity	Pain
Compatibility	Lethargic
Sacrifice	Lack of Confidence
Energy	Insecurity
Sharing	Reluctant
Caring	Rigid
Humble	Over Confidence
Meditate	Proud

(This chapter is for everyone to score more and correct themselves. And to be known as Deva's /Asura's)

PASSION AND COMPASSION

We know what passion is hence it is not very difficult to understand what compassion may be. Passion means a state of biological fever it is hot. You are almost possessed by biological, unconscious energies, you are no longer your own master, you are just a slave.

Compassion means you are no more a slave, you are a master. Now you function consciously.

Passion is lust, compassion is love. Passion is desire, compassion is desirelessness. Passion is greed, compassion is sharing.

Passion wants to use others as means, compassion respects others as end an end to himself.

Passion keeps you tethered to earth, to mud and you never become a lotus.

Compassion makes you a lotus. You start rising above the muddy world of desires, greed, and anger. Compassion is transformation of your energies. When all these energies are not wasted you become full. A great delight arises in you. "Compassion is the ultimate transformation of pas sion. You are in passion, but you go on thinking that you are right as you are. You go on defending yourself. And anything that disturbs your comfortable, mechanical life. You go against, you love to be alone, you love to meditate."

"Be passionate but one day finally you will love to be com passionate".

LEARN TO FAIL

We think failure is bad. It is not. It's good. No its great.

There can be no success without failure. Its just part of the process.

There companies and people who have reached the heights of success are the same ones that have failed the most often. You need to fail to win. And the faster you fail, the more quickly you'll learn precisely what you need to do to win. So fail fast. Outfail the competition. Outfail the person you once were.

"Only those who dare to fail greatly can ever achieve greatly".

A kid asked Swami Vivekanand "Sab kuch kohne se Jyada bura kya hai?"

Swamiji replied "Woh umeed khona, jiske Bharose par hum sab kuch vapas pa saktehai".

But after saying so I feel it is necessary to tell about failure is nothing but the repetition of the same act again and again and not learning from the past and not correcting the present leads to the next failure. If you start learning from the failure it becomes the steps to your success. And every failure in life is like a step ahead to your success. So fail faster, learn faster and be successful!

Happy Success!

SUFFERING

One of the most deeply hidden reasons for suffering is that you may be enjoying it. For example Falling ill can become a source of pleasure if it gets you the attention and care you have been craving for. In the same way as a seed has to rupture before plant can grow and blossom, intense suffering can rupture your ego and leave you open and vulnerable to transformation. Suffering has tremendous potential to integrate and transform us. Suffering is not a state of mind. It is not a event in your life. It is your response to a event. Never curse the pain or the person, inflicting the pain on you. Instead take the opportunity to use it as a blessing, watch objectively, and cut the root of the pain. Pain can be a great teacher if you allow it to be. If you properly research the cause and effect of pain with in you, it can turnout to be the biggest turning point in your life.

Every suffering is like a seed and caterpillar, like seed suffering can propel you to become a plant and blossom and caterpillar suffering can propel you to rupture and fly like a colourful butterfly!

Be Blissful!

INTENSITY

Intensity is not an emotional when you are intense, one part of it may be emotional. Intensity should become a quality in you. If you are talking let intensity be there. In your relationships, in your decisions, in your desires, even in your fears, be intense without escaping from this moment. Intensity does not depend on the nature of work or action. It can be as complex as running a billion dollar company or as simple as cleaning the floor. It is not 'what' but the 'how' that is important. Intensity means Radiating the energy that does not create any conflict inside and outside. Intensity is intensely being inside you. Intensity flows smoothly and yet strongly.

INTENT

An desire, an idea, an intention with emotional desire is called intent. To do something from bottom of the heart. If you are passionate about something then the whole universe will help you to make it happen. If your efforts are in one direction and the desire is in opposite direction of your stand then it will not workout and your intent will remain unfulfilled. So pay attention to the goal and focus with consistent e orts, sacrifice to your emotional and physical quest, give up some pleasures and take some short term pains to materialise your intent with lots of effort inputs without diverting focus you will be a receiver at the end of it. And finally you turn the tables around.

RESENTMENT

The person concerned, perceiving, injustice, wrongs or in gratitude nurtures a vague hope that his antagonism (op position) and intimidation (forcefully) would bring change of heart on the other person or situation. But this imagined 'cure' is worse than the disease. This unabated resentment is a deadly poison to spirit making happiness impossible and uses up tremendous energy, which could go into accomplishment. Such resentments are manifest signs of self image of not just a "pitiful person, a victim, who was meant to be happy," but also who needs unfavourable and hostile situations around his as alibis and excuses to justify this self image chosen for himself.

Resentment arises due to various reasons:

missing of opportunities,

difficult times faced earlier,

facilities denied or disappointments,

annoyance over unfairness all around.

A very common manifestation of such resentments or grudges, however is anger over ingratitude or lack of appreciations. These damaging feelings even were justified, have to be erased through comprehension

Of certain truths. Forget them and forgive them, you will be blessed twice. Don't feel restless, Be Blissful, and Be Happy!

"Make a mind which never minds,
Make a heart which never hurts,
Make a touch which never pains,
and make a relation which never ends."

HURT

Hurt starts with the habits which irritates, the way you eat, the way you talk, the way you look, the way you respond. Irritation becomes the cause of hurt. Initially the irritation which you hold on to your feelings and start hating the person and by saying you hurt me. Anything starts with irritation and if you don't resolve the same, you start judging people, by labeling like childish, immature, rude, clever, noncommittal, dominative, etc. and it grows into anger and thereby start arguments, conflicts, differences, then no conversations, then the hurt is so deep you stop talking to each other.

PAIN

When you are hurt you develop pain and sufferings and strain yourself, you start thinking, your emotional pattern gets disturb and stop focussing on work and resulting in no creativity, no energy, no enthusiasm in business resulting in failures. And while all this is going on the child's are the most effected victims of the hurt & pains which we are passing it on to them and they start adapting the same pattern without love and affection they growup serious in nature. And with lack of confidence & happiness. "Every painful story has a successful ending. Accept the pain & get ready for success".

And

"Every successful person has a painful story, then you need not worry you are also one."

PRINCIPALS OF BUSINESS

A Attention, Administration, Advertisements, Association, Ambience, Audit.

B Branding, Broadminded, Buying capacity, Banking, Balance sheet,

C Costing, Coordination, Customer care, Cooperation, Correspondence, Confidence,

Courageous, Considerable, Counseling, Clarity, Clear, Clean.

D Discounts, Delivery, Duty, Development, Duties, Dealers, Distributors.

E Ethics, Enthusiasm, Exhibitions, Extra Time, Extra

Cautious, Exemptions,

F Fair, Fearless, Fees, Fire Equipped, Fuel, Filtration, Filing, Formula.

G Genuine, Guarantee, Guidance, Government Guide lines, Graphs,

H Honesty, Human Resources, Hardship, HiProfile, Humble,

I Integrity, Incentives, Internship, International, Ideology,

J Joint Venture, Joint Meeting, Judicious, Judgemental, K Kind, Knowhow, Knowledge,

L Labour oriented, Lasting Relations, Long Lasting, Leverage, Loans, Licences,

M Morales, Motivation, Meetings, Marketing, Maintenance,

N Negotiations, Nice,

O Operations, Occasional, Overflow, Overhead, Office

P Principles, Payments, Purchases, Prompt, Publicity, Presentations, Packing, Profits, Pricing, Productions.

Q Quality, Quantity, Quotations, Quarrelessness,

R Research, Right, Renewals, Recycling, Registrations, Records, Resources.

S Secrecy, Sales, Schemes, Security, Skills, Subsidy, Salaries, Statistics, Size, Shape, Strength, Style, Shine, Sincerity, Statements.

T Timely Commitments, Target, Trust, Taxes, Technology, Trade Fairs, Training.

U Ultimate, Uniform, Uniqueness, User Friendly, Understanding.

V Validity, Velocity, Volume, Vehicles, Visiting cards, Visiting time,

W Workmanship, Work oriented, Workaholic, Water Re source, Wastage,

X Xerox, Xlinked dominant inheritance, Xlinked recessive inheritance

Y Yearly,Yield,Yardstick

Z Zeal, Zero, Zodiac

This are not words, this are the qualities, and responsibilities of a Good Administration who has to take care of so many subjects while administrating, therefore he is the Gem of the country who generates revenues, generate employment, gives taxes & duties, pay's interest to the bankers and enriches the flourishment of the distributors and dealers, takes care of the customers taste & choice, maintains stocks, maintains books of records, com plies govt policies of state and India. I therefore salute the administrator who takes so much of pains and gives his best efforts, keeping his family aside and leaves the pleasures of the world to serve you, from the early morning till the midnight. Truly Aspiring!

RELATIONSHIP

Needless to say parents contributes to form a Relation Father, mother, in laws but this is only 1/6th part of the share. To know more how the total share pattern of the entire relationship circle look like:

1. Parents Father, mother, in laws.
2. Spouse wife.
3. Relatives, Friends, Colleagues.
4. Children's
5. Self
6. Authority Senior in post.

CAUSES OF DETERIORATED RELATIONSHIP. Expectations, Lack of Respect, Conflicts, Lack of Connections, Lack of Communication, Feel Hurted, Feel Rejected, Feel Dejected, Feel Hatred, Confrontations, Frustrations, Depression.

And irritativeness in the Relations are the major causes of Deteriorated Relationships. "Trust is the base of every relation. A small mistake can change its entire meaning missing letter 'T' in Trust can 'Rust' the relations.

POWER OF BONDING RELATIONSHIP

If this area is strong enough, no crisis, no recession, no economy failures, nothing can affect you unless and until you have a strong bond in the family you will never come up in the life because it is the only ones will encourage you, nurture you, hold your hands to make your project a success and rest will try to destruct and create obstacles in the path. So, please give lots of time to relationship, by doing so you are not wasting time but you are ploughing and cultivating which will grow and gives you the fruits of affection and attachment, a strong hand to hold whenever you need it, this will lightened your stress, frequently talking to them will encourage you to perform well and in your daily tasks and improve your performance day by day, they will correct you where you are misguided or mislead by your opponents. Relationships are the nature's gift it is not by your choice but it is always the choice of the God so try to respect the gift of God Love them from bottom of the heart!

Quote : The Real measure of relation is not when two people like each other , it's when one ignores and the other continues loving with a silence till the end.

BREAKTHRU & BREAKDOWN FINANCES

Every person must involve, indulge in creating wealth or generating it is a intensely religious act. But at the same time making money is sin which is only possible in gambling, horse racing, forward trading, or other bad habits of making money. (Mcx, cricket; etc).

Wrong investments in wrong ventures, real estates, wrong people leads you to debts and will create breakdown finances. Rolling or rotating the money wisely is called a breakthru finances situations. Right emotions will bring you right contacts, wrong emotions will bring you wrong contacts and wrong habits of making money and results in breakdown emotions. And breakdown emotions start conflicting inside is nothing but the fear inside, blaming others, lack in confidence. In every second 50,000 cells die and are produced as we think they develop in the same line and then multiplies creating an depression like situation. Have a right emotion without a conflict or guilt, you will be high in the air, you will be a different person in you, a different individual to whom people like admiring, adoring, and liked by one and all.

Quote:" A Hardearned handfull of money is worthier than a bag full of Dollars won in a bet"

"Never lose your value for some sake of money because money may come and go, but it comes to value it can't be regained back and you may loose your dear ones"

"No Assets is not a problem , having liabilities is the biggest problem"

"No Liability is the biggest Assest"

Be Assetful !

MIND IS A SINNER

We are the creators of our thoughts, our feelings and our emotions. This are the three elements which disturbs you and hurt you, if you are taking them deep into the heart then assume it you are flown away by the creations of mind. We must protect them by shielding ourselves by saying that it is not me who can disturb by the thoughts or feelings, it is not me who can be flown away by the emotions, because I am soul and all this are the creations of mind. Mind is a sinner not me. Soul is sacred and serene, whereas thoughts, feelings and emotions are dreadful diseases generated by mind. So be careful don't allow them to nurture them in you, eradicate them by meditating, shielding by chanting "OM SHANTI OM" then you are fully protected from inner as well as outer criticism or guilt. Look as if you are an Odeon to the drama and watch every person as an character, don't try to change them, nor try to judge them, be an patient Odeon and enjoy the play by feeding them in your consciousness.

"To handle yourself use your mind, and to handle others, use your heart."

DETERMINATION

We find people who literally wander through life. They simply accept whatever fate brings them. A few may succeed by accident, but the most suffer through a lifetime of frustration and unhappiness. This is not for them but it is for those who have determination to succeed and willingness to devote the time and effort necessary to achieve success. To start an action plan for the rest of your life focus on the purpose and generate new ideas about yourself and future. Your attitude also contributes to succeed in achieving your goal. When our attitude is right, we realise that opportunity is always under our feet, we don't have to go anywhere, all we need to do is recognise it. Now put your character, integrity, good values, and positive attitude and work or adapt in practical theories of doing things, and have the right feelings, right relationships and put your efforts, a focussed determination and intense a result oriented, purpose driven, massive action plan, time bounded, lots of grace, and this determines your determination. And with this determination you are bound to succeed! "Everything is prewritten and nothing can be rewritten, thinking that we spend our days waiting for the ideal way to appear in front of us, but what we forget is that ways are made by walking not by waiting."

CERTAINITY & UNCERTAINITY

Certainty Risk Uncertainty

Certainty is nothing but a type of feeling, if you are certain it means you are comfortable, safe and secured, but vice versa feeling of certainity is insecurity, fearfulness, uncomfortable (uncertainity) life does not come with anything certain, change is the law of life, but challenge is an aim of life. So you have to challenge the changes but don't change the challenges. Changes happens does not entail time is second changes happen. Life is like a ball, the deeper you fall the higher you bounce back.

Nothing in this world is going to be as per your wish, it re quires proper planning, meticulous efforts, to keep everything in place. (certain) but certainly certainity is the key to happiness, but it has to craved for it by building your thoughts like every brick counts when we build a house, to build a good character every thoughts counts, so be positive and feed the mind daily with the positive thoughts.

The most important factor to keep certainity, do not make any small or big decisions on the basis of your mood. A mood is a dangerous state of mind because it can crush the reason under the weight of feelings. Always whatever decision you take in life musty be reasonable, less risky, less expectations, more practical it should be, otherwise extra hopes will get you more disappointments and uncertainty.

A single wrong decision could make your life miserable. Lifes critical decisions are to be evaluated before you decide. The process of evaluation should include the following things : 1. What am I doing, 2. What the result might be, 3. Will I be successful? Those who ignore the evaluation process are to have failure, or you may be deceived.

If you are deceived once and if you fail once, it does not matter, but if it is happening again and again then you are a fool and you alone are held responsible for your mistakes and therefore learn from failure and correct them for not repetition again in life. If you start learning from failures, the failures becomes your step to success. Those who stare at the past have their backs turned to the future thereby making your every single decision however small or big, more important or less important give a second thought to it and proceed uncertainity will disappear from your life or say certainity will prevail in your life and back to first paragraph certainity is nothing but a feeling of comfort ability, safety, and security and insecurity, fear fullness and uncomfortable feelings would disappear from your life forever. "Be certain in life"!

CONFIDENCE

When you start up any project or any work, you should known what you are doing and you should do with utmost interest and intensity and if you are following this then you are confident. But vice versa if you are starting any thing new without any knowledge about what you are going to do, and if you are not putting your mind without any interest than it is surely brings you lack of confidence. And if you are doing any venture without evaluation only with presumption and assumption and you are doing with a purpose of show off in society or the trade then surely it is your over confidence. Confidence brings success; lack of confidence brings humiliation and over confidence brings failures.

Confident comes by proper focus, 100% efforts total survey of the project and meticulous planning with action plan and time frame will surely give you confidence to tackle the obstacles in your venture, a strength to fight back to your opponents, to give everybody a shock on your successful achievements. So be confident and make your dreams into reality and raise upto to the challenges face boldly with instinct and righteous decisions without any conflicts in mind and clarity in your thoughts!

BE CONFIDENT..!!

ABOUT MYTHS OF PLANETS, VASTHU

Universe is with several solar systems. And one solar system with so many planets, movement of planets Rotation, Revolution and creates rays which effects our mind and thereby our thoughts and thoughts into action and the result are the reaction of our actions. Alpha and beta rays or say positive or Negative, or say malefic or benefic rays accordingly the body system functions and feels as per the reflections of the rays. Generally the energy produced by the movements of the planet from one place to another. It creates changes, cosmic energies which are good & bad, favourable & unfavourable, auspicious & adverse influences on the natives therefore the astrology is the science of movement of planet and calculations which evaluates the good and bad period coming ahead as per the movement calculations.

Vasthu is the science of air, water, earth, fire, elements. The flow and directions of the air, water the elevation and slopes of earth. The frequency of the waves as per universe system to flow with the universe the measure adapted would be beneficial and does not create any obstacles and not disturb the waves frequencies, thus helping to get maximum and be benefited by it scientifically is called Vasthu shastra which was followed by Vishwakarma, the architect and Engineer of the Hindu Gods. Hence the concept of Vasthu has become the tradition in India.

LIVE WITH PRIDE, NOT WITH PROUD

Living with pride is great, the conscious mind knows. Pride in other words signifies Dignity, humility, honor, humble. If you are doing whatever is touched by your heart that is pride, like if you are nursing your ailing mother caring your aged father, loving your wife and children, respecting your religious traditions, talking with humbleness to your colleagues, and honouring your mentors or teachers, it is pride.

Living with Proud is exhibiting your power, position, wealth, knowledge and appearances. Proud in other words is misuse of the gift of God Showed on you. If you are not conscious mind it means you are in subconscious mind which arise when you are over drunk. Proud is more or less dangerous intoxicant it could lead to fatals. Excess of drink or excess of power, excess of misuse of knowledge to fool others is fooling yourself. So it is better to be smart to be, rather than to be extra smart.

Anything in excess is dangerous, be in a conscious state of mind and live your life with pride instead of falling on roads after high intoxicants. Live a life with dignity & humility, you will be elevated to great heights!

NO ONE IS A BORN BILLIONAIRE

According to the world's hundred richest people today, 27 are heirs and 73 are self made, of the self made, 18 have no college Degree, and 36 are children of poor parents, but some billionaires had neither a degree nor wealthy parents. In other words super achievers are not born, they are self made people. It is not external favour that makes one a super achiever, but one's own struggle. Super achievement is not got through inheritance, but is self acquired success.

No one is a born a billionaire, but everyone is potential billionaire. It is the unfolding of one's own potential that makes one a billionaire or super achiever. Nature does not discriminate between one person and another nature gifts come to everyone equally. It is other receiver himself who either utilizes them or not.

So called deprived persons are in fact privileged persons. Their state of deprivation serves as inner motivation when they see others are progressing it creates a strong incentive in their minds. It is this incentive that makes a person, super. It articulates a strong urge in the individual to make something of his life.

Any state of deprivation brings about a kind of brain storming which enhances inner spirit. They enter the world of competition working to their full capacity they develop the spirit of do or die. It is this spirit that leads them to success.

There is a saying that "Mr. X was born with a silver spoon in his mouth". This kind of birth creates a kind of contentment in the concerned person, and this kind of contentment kills motivation. While a silver or a golden spoon, develops a kind of discontent ought to activate one's mind and trigger a fire within one to do hard work.

You can seldom find a family who started it's history with a treasure of gold and diamonds. Forever the treasure of gold is a phenomenon of the future, not of the present. Every family initially started its history from rags and not from riches. The story of rags to riches is not the story of exceptional persons, but it is the story of every successful family or successful person.

One who is born in a state of affluence could become intellectually dwarfed, while one who is born in poor circum stances could emerge on intelligent giant.

The law of nature are greater than everyone and everything else. They are eternal: they cannot be changed. The law of nature in this regard says that it is not else but effort, not facility but difficulty that makes achievers out of ordinary people. So the future is full of hope and opportunity Go and Get it!

LEARN TO LEARN

Learning has no ages, no boundaries, nor any ending, learning should be cultivated as a habit, must be thirsty to know more. Have curiosity to learn whatever, whenever you can. In any field learning should be a process if cultivated as a habit. It is knowledge and knowledge is always wisdom.

If you are a self employed or a employed, if you are a Doc tor or a Engineer, if you are a Politician or a Bureaucrat Learning only always pays back. It costs nothing and pay backs in abundant, if you are a wise planner and a Economist you will see the chart and graphs going up it can be monetary gain or can result in growth and development of the society from the process of learning. Paying back to the society is always appreciated. Appreciation brings recognition and recognition brings followers.

So, first be a follower first and the rest will follow. To learn you can surf, you can read, you can write you can listen, you can think, you can evaluate and finally you will be able to compile and make history.

And if you think learning is costly it is better to be a bank rupt rather than it is better to be a fool!

Inventions are the result of curiosity and knowing more and more without food and sleeping nights, with lots of day dreams with passion to do something will ultimately result in something "Do Something, something will hap pen, and do nothing, nothing will happen" always be with a great appetite to learn, be curious, be thoughtful, be creative, be fearless, be keen to know more and more you will be worthy. And if you are worthy than life is worth living, if you are content you are conscious, and if you are conscious you are close to source and back to God head. Learning always begins from the day we come into the world with closed hands and it continues every day till the final day of your journey back with opened hands. Close hands are givers and opened hands are takers and don't be a taker, be a giver. Giving is always bigger than taking. So think big, do big, learn big, give big, dream big, and from big to bigger and finally the biggest!

LACKING IS ALWAYS FAILURE

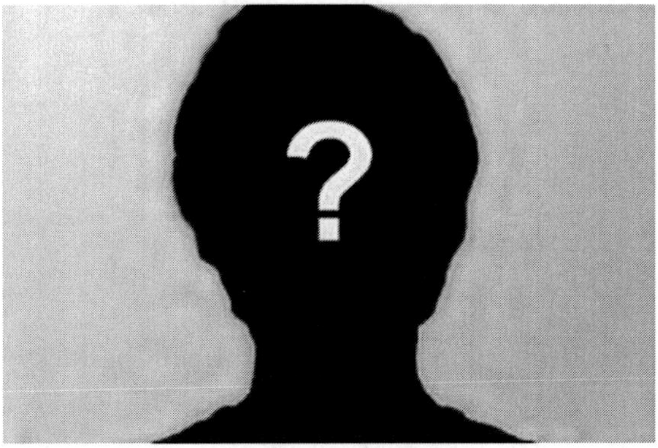

An entrepreneur who has succeeded not because he had surplus money, Business does not only run on money criteria. The days have gone, putting capitals in the Business is no more a criteria. T h e present trend of new entrepreneur is without bank balance are making millions, but if you lack money no problem but don't lack in the following criteria's:

1. Lack in full proof survey of the project
2. Lack in meticulous planning about the project
3. Lack in determination & confidence is the project
4. Lack in team spirit and timeless e ort for the project
5. Lack in present ability of your product.

6. Lack in approach to your customer
7. Lack in accountability of the finances
8. Lack in administration & management
9. Lack in communication skills.
10. Lack in quality & timely delivery
11. Lack in upgradation of technology
12. Lack in exposure of the company
13. Lack in Environment systems
14. Lack in customer satisfaction
15. Lack in research & Development
16. If you don't lack then you will be lucky, and people will recognize you as a leader. So don't worry, go ahead, an idea can change your life !

IMAGE IS NOT BY DEFAULT

Any person or company or a brand is not created in a short while. Image is not by default, it is the blue print of your impression created. A person image is built by the appearance, the way you walk, the way you talk, the way you dress, the way you smell, the way you take decisions, the way you react to the situations, the way you participate in a social gathering, the way you use your accessories. The impressions you have been doing in the past is your image in the present.

Company or a brand is like a child for 1000 days or say three years. You have to nurture it with care, with a great patience, develop it, transfrom it, maintain it, continue it, market it, promote it, and if you complete thousand days then it means you have created a brand image. Now your product is familiar, and the product is saleable, the product is worth it, the product is appreciable in the market. The appreciation is nothing but a brand image built in three years which now you will have to maintain it with the same quality which was appreciated by the customer. You have a choice to rename the product or change the packing of the product but not the content.

Happy Branding !!

DARE ARE THOSE WHO KNOW TO LOVE THEMSELVES

Loving any other is the easiest job, but loving self is the job of the bold. And who dare are those who know to love themselves, may not be loved by all but they crave themselves-in criticism or appreciation, in breakthru finances or breakdown finances, in situations under control or situations beyond control they over shine one and all they may be having lots of pains but they will not reveal anything and start to share your problems and try to find out the solutions for your problems, they may be confused on their path of life but they will be ready to guide you through your path if you feel you are confused. Loving self is selfishness, loving self is taking pain of others and not of self, loving self is not taking but only giving, loving self is very broader in perspective and not narrow, loving self is sacrifice and not comforts, loving self is hunger and feeding others, loving self is lotus and not cactus, loving self is desert and not green lash, loving self is devotion and not hatred, loving self is peace and not impatient, loving self is darest of all the bolder things in the world. So dare to love yourself.

PUPPET SHOW THE WORLD

Yes, if you are thinking how the world can be puppet show, you are going right. To know more precisely read this First is the puppet show consists of characters which are good and bad, second is the total show is managed on strings and proper timing to give its best effects third is the architect, creator and player of the show. In the same way the world also plays. Each and everyone is a character in itself. All are managed by timing from kids to executives, housewives to servants, engineers to doctors, astrologers to tarot readers, but the only thing common in both the show is the architect, creator, and player. He is the back the curtain, he is never seen, he is never appreciated, he is never exposed to the public. He is the key player of the entire show He is invisible, He is known as Ram, Rahim, Nanak, Jesus in places from North to South and East to West, for him their is no boundaries, no caste, no creed, no favour or disfavour, he as per the character he gives the actions and as per actions he is been awarded good or bad, king or beggar, weak or bold, ugly or beautiful, soft or hard. The creation is his choice, he chooses the character, he chooses the place, he chooses the time of entry, he chooses the action, he chooses the qualities, he chooses the exit from the show. Isn't it very strange but true, we are puppet in the hands of master and our strings are controlled by him and therefore we have no choice of anything to choose, so let us enjoy playing a character in the show, who knows when is our exit is from the show.

That's true, that's life!

INNOCENCE IS ADORABLE

Innocence is pure as water, innocence is like a lotus, innocence is like a peacock, innocence is like a incense stick.

To magnify why Innocence is pure as water it is soft and flow swiftly as per the way and never stagnants at a place it keeps going and mixes up with the lakes, rivers and seas but never changes its attitude.

Innocence is like a lotus in the mud, no mud slings can stay on it because it is very fragile and stable therefore it floats with the big base leaves slowly steadily moves to the edges without any struggle or force.

Innocence is like a peacock, a colourful bird very beautiful and dances in the forest without any reasons, and it is only the purest of all liked by God of all community Nanak, Krishna, Dargah. The male peacock weeps and the female peacock takes the drop for conceiving and sacrifice is their reproduction cycle – Therefore purest of all, all loved by all. Innocence is like a Incence stick you light at any place it will give you the same smell, whether you place it the pooja room, or the bedroom, at the bar or Dargah. The smell never changes as per places, the duration does not change, nor the appearance changes changes are only external but not internal so be innocent, be pure, be soft, be beautiful, be stiff but always never forget your qualities.

HOW HARD IT IS TO BE A FATHER

Don't take me wrong by the heading of the chapter. The man's mind is full of womanity and about sex. But it is not what you are thinking. It is about nurturing your son from the day one from his birth, you start caring, loving, and buying each and everything for his comfort and joy without his demand. From napy to nipple, from dress to shoes, from bed to cradle to make him feel comfortable, beautiful and joyous always. Now a days growing a baby is a hard and costly job, from oils to soaps, creams to nutrients, from medicines to syrups you cut down your bud get of comforts and sacrifice. Thereafter you sacrifice your budget for his schooling, books, dress, fees, shoes, then after some years you cut down more your budget for his colleges, his jeans, T-shirts, pocket moneys, movie and games.

Then after he gets a good job it is his time to pay back and he starts with father "Don't try to disturb me", "Don't try to dictate me", "Don't try to interfere in my life", then after he is married he says "Don't try to indulge with our family" and last but not least he says "Leave us alone".

There the poor father what he gets in pay back after his life long sacrifices and cutting down his budget of his comforts, only abuse, abuse, abuse, and nothing else and finally at this old age he is left with no option and looks for a home for age and lives his rest life..

DAD A SMILE FOR YOU

A great man who spares his life Hides his feelings ....

Ignores his happiness .... Accepts the pain .... Forgets his comforts .... Struggles in work ....

To make us to live comfortably and happy in our life with out any struggle, so wear a smile for you dad which costs nothing, only a smile and makes him feels rejuvenated, and it will distress him. A small smile can do big wonders for him, he will be charged with more enthusiasm to work to make you feel more and more happier only at the cost of a smile and nothing else!

SO

SMILE PLEASE AT NO COST

TOTALLY 100% FREE

MOTHER THE ULTIMATE GOD

In reality no one in the world has seen God, we have been only told about him that he was like that, he did this and that and his name is so and so. But in the reality the God you have seen, you have felt her warmth, you have been fed by her with utmost care and hide, because she loved you more than herself. When you were young she slept in your wet to make you sleep in the dry. She takes the pain for nine complete months and thereafter the whole life till she is alive. When you come drenched in the rain, brother scolded, father warned, sister shouted, but mom while dry ing the sons hair said "Stupid rain! Couldn't you stop till my child comes home?" When you grown up and married and after you became a father still you are a son to her and when you come home from your business in the night wife asked about the sale, son asked about the profit and father asked about the payments, mother lastly asked

"Have you had your lunch?". This is called mother The Utimate God.

"Azeez bhi Woh hai naseeb bhi Woh, duniya ki bheed me kareeb bhi Woh, Iske Aashirwaad se chalti Zindagi, Khuda bhi Woh Aur Taqdeer bhi Woh hai!"

"Koi rasta nahi duva ke siva, Koi sunta nahi kuda ke siva,

Maine bhi zindagi ko karib se dekhahai, Mushkil me koi saath nahi deta, MAABAAP KE SIVA!"

Love and respect your real God and in turn they will not ask for anything else from you.

"Is pyaar me bewafai ka jarokha nahi hota, har rishta itna

Anokha nahi hota,

fana kardo zindagi maabaap ke kadmo me, Quki yahi who pyar hai jisme

Dhokha nahi hota."

"Mere Gunaho ko wo maaf kar deti hai, Bahut gusse me hoti hai to bhi pyar deti hai, Labo pe uske hameysha duva hoti hai,

Aisi sirf "Maa hoti hai".

Zindagi mein do logo ka bahut khayal rakhna,

1. Woh joh tumhari jeet ke liye bahut kuch hara ho (pa pa).
2. Woh jisko tumne har dukh me pukaro ho (maa).

Yeh toh Sach hai ke Bhagwan Hain,
Hain magar phir bhi anjaan hain,
Dhartee pe roop MaaBaap ka,
Yeh vidhaata ki pehchaan hain

MaatPita tum mere sharan gahoon mein kiski,
Tum bin aur na dooja aas karu mein jiski

SISTERS THE POWER HOUSE

You are the fortunate if God had blessed you with a sister and the more sisters you are more fortunate to have them. You are blessed with his abundance. If you have elder sister then she is known as second mother and if the sisters are younger then they are reason for your happiness. They are always there through out the good and bad phases of life without any regrets, they always stand by you even if you are right or wrong and defend you. They are the power house, they encourage and motivate you, they simply be lieve in you with blind eyes and never can hear anything adverse about you however it is whatever it is they stand before you who ever is against you. Though they may be younger to you but at times come when they feel you are not taking care of yourself they become your grandma and feed you forcibly. They treat you like the father and really its very fortunate to have such good daughters (sisters) when in love you call them beta (daughter) more or less like. Nothing more is precious in the world, nothing more is priceless in the world, nothing more is prestigious to have the sisters who are caring, loving, always there to share your emotions, always there to understand your feelings, always there to make you feel as if "you are the best". Thank you God for such beautiful and priceless gift to me. These are my assets of life. God give me strength that I does not become an liability to them. Love you all from the bottom of the heart!

BEING ADVENTUROUS MEANS FALL ON FACE

Life is itself full of adventures ,but the lust of more is dangerous you might have seen the hoardings on the Highways saying "Speed thrills but kills" that true but we do not follow in practical life hence fall on face. Two young girls, Laukika and Samantha set off on an adventure. Both of them had completed their formal education and before venturing into their respective Samsaric enterprises, they thought of taking a break to contemplate life. Laukika was so overwhelmed with the idea of hedonistic idea of journeying and her own enthusiasm that she said to her friend. "I am going to jump into the river, Samantha and be carried along with its great energies. Meet you later". So saying, she took the plunge, without waiting for her friend to respond Laukika enjoyed the initial adventure. At times the river frightened her, its strong current sweeping her along. But she dismissed her fears as she could now no longer see the shore. Laukika was euphoric and wanted more of the adventure. Forever engrossed in steadying herself from the speed of her journey. She managed mere fleeting glimpses of the beauty around her.

Now, the waves got bigger, the waters deeper, the river widened, the gusting became so forceful that she was thrown about, knocked about on the rocks all over, water and sand filled her nostrils and mouth, she was being bruised by the gravel and creatures in the river "Help me to the sore. Someone". She cried, but no one heard her. Those who did hear her could not do much as they were not in a position to help her and finally one large wave thrown her on her face to the shore. Meanwhile, Samantha had set out on the foot,. "I choose to walk down the river bank instead. I might be able to enjoy the vistas better this way". She had thought to herself before embarking on her journey. Many years passed The two friends met again. They hugged each other, happy to meet once again. Laukika admitted she did have her share of fun, but the journey had tired her out. Moreover she felt vacant inside. There was so much she wanted to do. She said but the sheer speed of her journey didn't permit her to take those liberties.

Samantha Spoke: "I too thought for long after you left me. Laukika I was tempted to follow you. The river looked enticing. But then, there was no hurry either I chose to walk down instead. I got to experience and enjoy the scenic offerings around the river. I marveled at the Sunrise and Sunset that were so different each day. The open blue sky was so reassuring as were the stars at night. I played with the countless butterflies and birds that filled the forest. I stopped to smell the forest and fainted with breath for the Kingfisher to dive into the water for a quick meal, and the Seagulls that flew over my head. I was tempted many times to plunge myself into the racing river, but would spend only a little time in the waters before drying myself on the warm rocks on the banks, read a book and resume my journey., The local people who collected firewood and fruits from the forest would invite me to their humble homes. I would play with their children and share with them simple tips on improving their health before bidding them goodbye. It has been an amazing journey.

The friends sat in silence, mulling over the choices they'd made and the experiences they'd been through.

YOU ARE UNIQUE

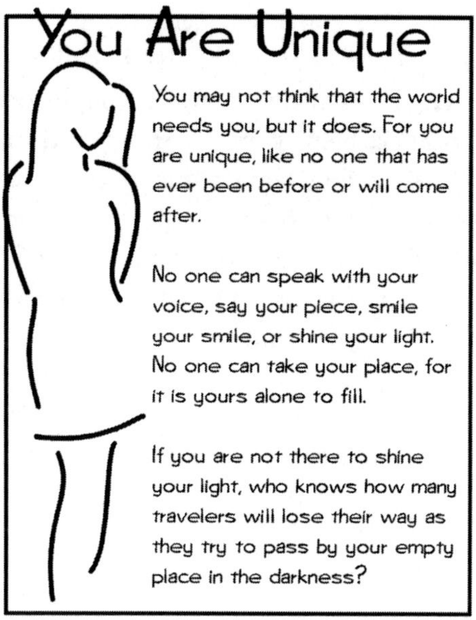

Cosmic light is the basis of all beauty and diversity in the universe, as well as of all biodiversity and life on earth. Each form of life is unique. Human beings the most evolved form of life, are most capable owing to especially evolved mind that controls the human phenomenon of being in Unison with cosmic powers of being an ally of the cosmos in its design of unfolding itself of creating new highs of creativity.

This uniqueness blossoming within every person is one the greatest wonders of universe light. This light writes the unique story of potential creativity in the mind of every one. What others have done so far, what other could not dare to do so far, you can do it. What specific thing you can do might be impossible for others to do. You can learn everything through your interaction with others, through attending classes in a University, through books and through media. Your common intellect helps you to learn everything you like to learn. But it is only the unique distribute nurturing itself within you which can help you invent, unfold and do something unique, something different from all others that you are a wonder in yourself. It is the unique attribute within you that can help you to reinvent yourself. It is the unique attribute shining within you can help you construct a new world and glitter within you and sparkle to new era of human creativity.

OPPORTUNITY

Doubtless, one who comprehends and applies the art of right timing, also seizing the opportunities, as they come, is also the one who divines that Supreme art of life and living.

What is actually opportunity The face of the God which is concealed and it has wings on its feet, it is always unrecognized when it comes to you. "It is because men seldom recognize this God when it comes to them. He flies away soon and once gone, never comes back".

It is only possible by seizing the moment by doing the right thing at the right time and in a right manner. Whereby one is able to make the best of available resources. Even timely anger, when channeled well and rightly, could serve to galvanise a working force or the human resources, where gentle persuasion may fail. Of course anger with onself, attended with a steely determination to make up could be highly rewarded. At the same time tactful inaction or silence in certain situation could prove more powerful than reactions or responding. A great lesson for life is contained in every aspect of life. We should have the urge to learn, but not to wait for the opportunities while resourceful person make them. In deed, opportunity often knocks just once.

Like an idea, this too has to be welcomed, entertained, nurtured and fashioned into a rewarding destiny.

The wish power and will power within, also rooted in effective and right timing, could regardless of delayed efforts, be restored to for substantial fulfillment, instead resorting to passive repentance or regrets over a dead past.

Forget the past, work on present an so will be the outcome of your future. Don't wait for opportunity, create one, by doing right thing, in right direction, in right way and at the right time. Imply your innovative ideas and convert into reality. This is opportunity Grab it !.

NEVER CHANGE THE THREE BARBER, COUNSEL, DOCTOR

Never change the three is also written in the Old Scripture of Hindu's. The reasons for doing so is explained to you one by one.

Barber: The barber is the person who makes over your looks, he is only the person who knows what suits you the best. What should be the size of your side locks as per your face, what should be the cut of your hairs and why? He is the person who decides and makes your appearance a pleasing personality, which is the first and foremost rule of a Gentleman.

ADVOCATE

Counsel: The Counsel is the person who knows about the mistake you have committed and proves that my client has not done anything wrong and proves you innocent. He knows the weakness of your opponent and keeps on hit ting on it with so many rules and sections which finally proves him guilty and you as innocent.

Doctor: The Doctor is the person who knows your body more than you. He knows what your body accepts and what does not. He knows what is your resistant capacity to which disease and which medicine suits you without any side effect to you while curing.

Therefore always respect the three and never ever think of changing them as per your convenient, or else it could get you humiliation, penalty, or fatalism in your life. Give your second thought for the three and you will know the importance of it and deep thinking will surely prove the point of explanations are true and correct.

THE 20 CAREFULLY CHOOSEN ONELINERS BY ROBIN SHARMA

1. Dream big. Start small. Act now.
2. Victims make excuses. Leaders deliver results.
3. Clarity breeds mastery.
4. Education is inoculation against disruption.
5. A problem is only a problem when viewed as a problem.
6. All change is hard at first, messy in the middle and gorgeous at the end.
7. If you are not scared a lot you are not doing very much.
8. Where victims see adversity. Extreme achievers see opportunity.,
9. The Project you are most resisting carries your greatest growth.
10. Small daily improvements overtime lead to stunning results.
11. Criticism is the price of ambition.
12. Potential unexpressed turns to pain.
13. Ordinary people love entertainment, extraordinary people adore education.
14. Our daily behavior reveals your deepest beliefs.
15. The only failure is not trying.

16. Focus is more valuable than IQ.
17. To double your income, triple your investments in self development.
18. Your excuses are nothing more than the lies your fears sold you.
19. An addiction to distraction is the end of your creative production.
20. Life is short. Be of use.

15 MOST PRECIOUS QUOTES BY ROBIN SHARMA

1. "The Reasonable man adapts himself to the world, the unreasonable one Persists in trying to adapt the world to himself. Therefore all progress depends on the unreasonable man".
2. "People who have achieved great success are not necessarily more skillful on intelligent than others. What separates them is their turning desire and thirst for knowledge. The more one knows, the more one achieves".
3. "Your most challenging Relationship carries with it the seed of your greatest growth. The Relationship that tests, frustrates, irritates the most actually is one of your greatest blessing".
4. "The Project that most scares you is the project you need to do first".
5. "Victims are frightened by the changes, leaders are inspired by the changes".
6. Your two primarily Assets: Your mental focus and your physical energy.
7. Excuses prevents us from taking action.
8. With more awareness you can make better choices with better choices you will see better results.
9. Complaining is worrying made verbal.,

10. The words you use in your subconscious mind. Rewire your beliefs.
11. Remember that critics are dreamers one scared.
12. Fears unfaced becomes your limits.,
13. Don't be the richest person in the graveyard, because health is wealth.
14. Life is short. The greatest risk is riskless living. And setting for a Average".
15. Worries destroy your physical body and creativity of mind.

SOME IMPORTANT DO'S AND DON'T

1. Avoid the three pool of water, forest and party. If unavoidable go for a while and come back.
2. Never make friends with people who are above or be low you in status, such friendship will never give you any happiness.
3. A person should not be too honest. Straight trees are cut first and honest people are screwed first.
4. Before you start some work, always ask yourself 3 ques tions
   1. Why am I doing it?
   2. What the results might be?
   3. Will I be successful?

   Only when think deeply and find satisfactory answers to this questions. Go ahead.
5. The biggest Guru mantra is never share your secrets with anybody. It will destroy you.
6. Once you start working on something, don't be afraid of failure and don't abandon it. People who work sincerely are the happiest.
7. Do not reveal what you have thought upon doing, but by wise council keep it secret being determined to carry it into execution.

8. In unfavourable situations surrender to your enemy, but when time favours break his head like a wet pot on the hard rock.
9. If your wife behaves like a mother in morning, by noon like a sister and by night like a prostitute Then you are lucky.
10. A book in the hand of a stupid is like a mirror in the hand of a blind.
11. If your son is a stupid then amassing of wealth is waste, and if your son is intelligent then also amassing the wealth is more waste.
12. If you are trying to please everybody, it means you are fooling yourself.
13. You will never reach your destination if you stop and throw stones at every barking dogs. Better keep biscuits and move on.
14. Everyone is good to you till you expect nothing from them, and you are too good to them only till you fulfill their expectations.
15. A servant is tested at the time of work, relatives at the time of suffering, friends in calamities and women dur ing the loss of wealth.
16. Separation from one's wife, lack of respect from friends and relatives, a balance of loan, service of an evil king, poverty, and a gathering of fools all these burn the body without fire.
17. Sita was kidnapped because of too much beauty, Ra vana was killed because of excess pride, King Bali was bound in ropes because of excess charity, therefore always shun excess in anything.

18. No official is above greed, one without desire is not fond of beauty, an intelligent person cannot be a sweet talker, and a straightforward cannot be a crook.

19. A wise man should never reveal the following: a loss of wealth, a worry bothering mind, faults of his household, having been made a fool by someone, and being humiliat ed.

20. One should be satisfied with following three: one's own wife, food, and money.

    One should be never satisfied with following three: one's study, penance and charity.

21. Whatever is given to an undeserving person ignoring the deserving one, would be like giving something to an ass ignoring a cow.

22. The greatest fear in the world is of the opinions of others, and the moment you are unafraid of the crowd, you are no longer a sheep, you become a lion A great roar arises in your heart, a roar of freedom!

23. "No one is above the law" and at the same time "No one is below it".

MORAL STORIES

We listen what we want to hear and not what is said.

A medical doctor was giving a lecture on how the liquor is injurious to health and to prove this he had two glasses – one with distilled water and the other with alcohol in it. He put an earthworm into the distilled water it swam beautifully and came up to the top. He put another earthworm into the alcohol and it disintegrated in front of everyone's eyes. He wanted to prove that this was what alcohol did to the insides of our body. He asked the group that what was the moral of the story and a person from behind said, "If you drink alcohol you won't have worms in your stomach", and the spectator's laughed and he concluded the speech. The person saying was an selective listening – we hear what we want to hear and not what is being said so "please listen to what is not said and don't listen to what is said".

Luck will favour you if efforts are done.

A flood was threatening a small town and everyone was leaving for safe ground except for one man who said, "God will save me. I have faith". As the water level rose a jeep came to rescue him, the man refused, saying "God will save me. I have faith". As the water level rose further, he went up to the second floor of his house, and a boat came to help him. Again he refused to go, saying

"God will save me. I have faith". The water kept rising and the man climbed on to the roof, a helicopter came to rescue him, but he said, "God will save me. I have faith". Well, finally he drowned. When his soul reached the god, he angrily questioned, "I had complete faith in you, why did you ignore my prayer's and let me drown?" The Lord replied – "Who do you think sent you the jeep, the boat, and the helicopter"?

"It takes action, preparation, and planning rather than wasting, wandering, and wishing, to accomplish any goal in life by itself, relying upon luck or saying you have faith in God, he will favour you, elevate you one day without any efforts is a wrong myst.

There is no easy way to get food.

Once there was a lark singing in the forest. A farmer came by with a box full of worms. The lark stopped him and asked, "What do you have in the box and where are you going"? The farmer replied – that he had worms and that he was going to the market to trade them for some feathers. The lark said, "I have many feathers. I will pluck one and give it you and that will save me looking for worms". The farmer gave the worms to the lark and the lark plucked a feather and gave it in return. The next day the same thing happened and the day after day on and on until a day came that the lark had no more feathers. Now it could no longer fly to go hunting for worms, it started looking ugly and stopped singing and very soon it died out of hunger.

"The moral of the story is quite clear – what the lark thought was an easy way to get food turned out to be the tougher way after all". Many times we look for easier way, which really ends up being the tougher ways after.

WE ARE FAR BEHIND UNLESS WE ARE NOT PREPARED OR NOT DOING ANY ACTION.

A man bought a race horse and put him in a barn with a big sign, "The fastest horse in the world". The owner did not exercise the horse, nor trained to keep it fit and in good shape. He entered the horse in a race and it came last. The owner quickly charged the sign to "The fastest world for the horse", by inaction or not doing what should be done, people fail and they blame the luck.

FEAR ALSO MOTIVATES.

A company wanted to setup a pension plan. In order for the plan to be implemented, it needed 100% participation. Every one signed up except John. The plan made sense and was in the best interest of everyone. John's refused to sign was the only obstacle. John's supervisor and other coworkers had tried, without success, to persuade him to sign. The owner of the company called John into his office and said, "John, here is a pen and these are the papers for you to sign to enroll into the pension plan. If you don't enroll, you are fired this minute, and you will be out of the company. Right now." John took the pen signed the papers and while he was leaving the owner asked "John why he had not signed the papers earlier". John replied – "No one explained the plan quite as clearly as you did":

"If the fear of firing and removing from the company was not there in mind so he was reluctant to sign as soon as the fear motivated him he signed without any questions, because he was the only bread & butter winner for the family."

CHOOSE EITHER NEGATIVE OR POSITIVE FROM THE SAME – SOURCES:

A story of two brothers. One was a drug addict and he drunk frequently beat up his family. The other was a very successful businessman who was respected in the society and had a wonderful family. How could two brothers raised by the same parents, brought up in the same environment, be so different? The first brother was asked – "What makes you do what you do? You are a drug addict, a drunk, and you beat your family. What motivates you? He answered, "My father. My father was a drug addict, a drunk and beat his family. What do you expect me to be? That is what I am". The second brother was asked, "How come you are doing everything right? What is your source of motivation?" And guess what he said? "My father. When I was a little boy, I used to see my dad drunk and doing all the wrong things. I made up mind that, that is not I wanted to be". So the moral of the story both the brothers derived their motivation from the same source, but one was using it positively and the other negatively.

A GREEDY PERSON WOULD END WITHOUT ENJOYING ANYTHING.

A wealthy farmer was once offered all the land he could walk in a day provided he returned by sundown to the point at which he started. To get a head start, early the next morning the farmer started covering ground quickly because he wanted to get as much land as he could. Even though he was tired, he kept going all afternoon because he did not want to loose the once in a lifetime opportunity to gain more wealth. Late in the afternoon he remembered that the condition he had to fulfill to get the land was to get back to the starting point by sundowns. His greed had gotten him far from the starting point. He started his returning journey, keeping an eye on how close he was to sundown. The close it got to sundown, the faster he ran. He was exhausted and out of breath, and he pushed himself beyond the point of endurance. He collapsed upon reaching the starting point and died. He did make it before sundown. He was buried and all the land he needed was a small plot.

"There is a lot of truth in the story and a lesson to be learned, whether the farmer was wealthy or not, any greedy person would have ended the same way, at last!"

Think considerably for self as well as others too.

A ten year old boy went to an ice cream shop, sat at a table and asked the waitress, "How much is an ice cream cone? She said, "Seventy five cents". The boy started counting the coins he had in his hand. Then he asked how much a small cup of ice cream was. The waitress impatiently replied, "Sixty five cents". The boy said, "I will have the small ice cream cup". The boy ate his ice cream, paid the bill and left. When the waitress came to pick up the empty plate, she was touched. Underneath the plate were ten one cents coins left as the tip. The young boy had consideration for the waitress before he ordered his ice cream. He showed sensitivity and caring. He thought of others before himself.

So always show some considerations, courtesy and politeness attitude to others so they will care for you, love you, and respect you.

I FEEL HOW YOU FEEL, AND I UNDERST AND HOW YOU FEEL IS NOTHING BUT EMPATHY & SYMPATHY.

A boy went to the pet store to buy a puppy. Four puppies were sitting together, priced at $50 each. Then there was one sitting alone in a corner. The boy asked if that was from the same litter, if it was for sale, and why it was sitting alone. The store owner replied that it was a deformed one, and is not for sale. The boy asked what the deformity was. The store owner replied that the puppy was born without a hip socket and had a leg missing. The boy asked, "What will you do with this one?". The reply was it was it would be put to sleep. The boy asked if he could play with that puppy. The store owner said, "Sure". The boy picked the puppy up and the puppy licked him on the ear. Instantly the boy decided that was the puppy he wanted to buy. The store owner said, "That's not for sale!" The boy insisted and requested, the store owner agreed. The boy pulled out $2 from his pocket and ran to get $48 from his mother. As he reached the door the store owner shouted after him, "I don't understand why you would pay full money for this one when you could buy a good one for the same price". The boy did not say a word. He just lifted his left trouser leg and he was wearing a brace. The pet store owner said, "I understand. Go ahead, take this one". The boy showed was empathy – and store owner showed was sympathy.

HOW PEOPLE REMEMBER YOU AFTER YOUR DEATH.

About a hundred years ago, a man looked at the morning newspaper and to his surprise and horror, read his name in the obituary column. The newspaper had reported his death by mistake. His first response was shock. Am I here or there? When he regained his compromise, his next thought was to find out. What people had said about him. The obituary read, "Dynamite King Dies", and "He was the merchant of death". This man was the inventor of dynamite and when he read the words "Merchants of death", he asked himself, "Is this how I am going to be remembered? He decided that this was not the way he wanted to be remembered. From that day on, he started working towards peace. He, the Dynamite King, was Alfred Nobel and he is remembered today by the great Nobel prizes. Just as Alfred Nobel redefined his values, you should step back and do the same.

Is your life worth living.

A boy was drowning in a river and he shouted for help. A man passing by jumped in the river and saved the boy's life. As the man was leaving the boy said, "Thank you". The man asked, "For what"? The boy replied. "For saving my life". The man looked into the boy's eyes and said, "Son, make sure when you grow up that your life was worth saving.".

This is a wakeup call. It is time to think. Success without fulfillment is meaningless, unless there is a sense of meaning and purpose. Life is empty and unhappy regardless of how much prestige, money, or education you have.

The responsibility of parenting.

A Judge when sentencing a man for robbery, asked if he had anything to say. The man replied: "Yes, your honour, please sentence my parents to jail also". The Judge asked, "Why"? The prisoner answered, "When I was a little boy. I stole a pencil from school. My parents knew about it but never said a word. Then I stole a pen, they knowingly ignored it. I continued to steal many other things from the school and the neighborhood till it became an obsession. They knew about it, yet they never said a word. If anyone belongs in jail with me, they do".

He is right, although it does not absolve him of his responsibility, the question is did the parents do their job right? Obviously not. Giving choices to children is important, but choices without directions result in disaster. Complete mental and physical preparation is the result of sacrifice and self discipline.

"A tree can make one lakh match sticks, but one match stick can burn one lakh trees", in the same way a single wrong doing will one day become your habit and then character. So always culture the habit of educating your children what is wrong in life and what is right! Be in higher conscious state of mind!

INTERNAL MOTIVATION IS THE INNER GRATIFICATION, NOT FOR SUCCESS OR WINNING, BUT FOR THE FULFILLMENT THAT COMES FROM HAVING DONE IT.

Coach to a player – "Son how could I have been so wrong? I have never seen you play like this before. What happened? How did you play so well? I have no confident in you so I have kept you as the last player? How could you do this?

The boy replied, "Coach, my father is watching me today". The coach turned around and looked at the place where the boy's father used to sit. There was no one there. He said "Son, your father used to sit there when you came for practise, but I don't see anyone there today". The boy replied, "Coach, there is something I never told you. My father was blind, just four days ago, he died. Today is the first day he is watching me from above". Inerral motivation in the inner gratification, not for success or winning, but for the fulfillment that comes from having done it.

NEVER PUT A MASK, BE WHAT YOU ARE.

A young executive with poor self esteem was promoted, but he could not reconcile himself to his new office & position. There was a knock at his door. To show how important and busy he was, he picked up the phone and then asked the visitor to come in. As the man waited for the executive, the executive kept talking on the phone, nodding and saying, "No problem, I can handle that". After a few minutes he hung up and asked the visitor what he could do for him. The man replied – "Sir, I am here to connect your phone."

YOU ARE WHAT GOD MADE YOU TO BE, SO DON'T GET COMPLEX, LOVE YOURSELF AND SERVE THE MANKIND.

There was a potter was had two pots for him for getting the water for food & drink. Out of both the pots one had a little crack in it. The potter daily use to take the pots tied to the stick with two pots on both the sides. The pot which was without any crack use to abuse the cracked pot that "You are fit for nothing, nor you can give our master the full water for his hardship and your water gets leaked through out in the path". By listening daily the cracked pot one day thought that whatever my brother pot is saying is fact and I must end myself, so that the master shall make a new and good pot like the other pot. The next morning when the master went to pick up the pots for water the cracked pot told the master that "I have no worthiness nor useful to you so you better break me and make a new pot for yourself which will give you the full water". The master understood the feeling of the cracked pot and said let me show you something first and if you feel, you are correct I will break you. The master took both the pots to the pond and filled the pots with water and while his return journey to house he walked half the way and stopped and said – "Now listen I agree that the strong pot though gave me pot full of water but my other crack pot did not gave me pot full of water but he gave lush green grass throughout the path. A period ago there were thorny bushes here and pointed stones which use to pierce my legs and I use to bleed profusely daily but now, see my legs, I have no injuries anymore because by daily leaking water throughout the path the lush green grass has become my velvet passage and without any pain, I can do the job and at the same time how he is watering the grass to keep them green glowing. Now if you feel your are not fit for anything after going home I will break you. The cracked pot said "I am sorry, I was unable to know the comforts God gave you because of my weakness therefore forgive me and please do not break me I will be happy to serve you as I am.

Comparing and postponing the happiness will not allow you to enjoy the present.

A mother had two daughters and elder was studying in tenth and the younger was in eight. The younger daughter had an habit of comparing herself with her elder sister. One day when the elder sister passed her tenth exam and started her college, seeing the younger sister was not happy and the mother asked "Why are you not happy, your elder sister has passed tenth and joined college".?

She replied – "I will be happy only when I pass my tenth exam and when I will join college, because I love very colorful dresses and not this school uniform." Mother said, "My dear daughter for that you need to wait for two years because you are in eight".

She replied – "No problem, I am ready to wait till I pass my tenth and join the college". After two years passed her elder sister joined the degree college and the younger passed the tenth and joined the college but after joining the college she was not happy because she wanted to join degree like her elder sister and therefore she was not happy in her intermediate college. After three years her elder sister had completed the degree and the mother seen a alliance for her and marriage was fixed and the marriage day – her younger sister was asked by mother "Are you not happy, your sister is getting married". She replied – "No, I will be happy, when I complete by degree and I will be married". Two years passed the younger daughter also finished her degree and had an alliance and she was married. The elder daughter had given a birth to boy child and the mother and younger daughter visited the hospital after seeing the baby mother was very happy and "asked her younger daughter are you not happy your sister has given birth to such a beautiful boy". Then she replied "No. I will be happy. When I will give birth to the beautiful boy like sister has given". After a year she gave a birth to the child more beautiful then her sisters son. Many years passed and her mother also passed away, and one day when she stood before the mirror she noticed that her hairs have turned white the childrens have grown up and in comparison and by postponing the happiness she has come to an old age. Now, she was able to realise that by comparing her sister and postponing the happiness the life from thirteen to forties. Thereafter she stopped comparing herself with the sister and enjoyed each and every day of life with her husband and grown up childrens and thereafter they lived happily ever after.

Never be proud of anything or else you will be under the feet.

In a river bank there was a rock and a few meters away on one the plant there was a very beautiful flower. The flower use to laugh on the rock saying that how ugly you are and how incapable you are, the waves are hitting on you are you are unable to do anything. I really feel very pity for you. After somedays river dried up and the rocks very so black & soft the sculpture took it the home and made God statues and sold the same to the temples. The statues were installed and people came with flowers to the Deity and the priest use to put them to the feet of Deity. The rock (deity) even now never told anything to the flower and the flower understood that my proud of my beauty and laughing on someone else situation has bought him to the feet of the rock.